# *Witch Doctor*

## By

## Jessica Rougeau

*Witch Doctor* by Jessica Rougeau

Cover Art by: **Anthony D. Marsilio**

*Witch Doctor*

by **Jessica Rougeau**

**For Ashley**

*Witch Doctor* by **Jessica Rougeau**

# TABLE OF CONTENTS

Diorama - 6

King - 7

Special Guests - 8

Grave Gang - 9

Only Annual - 10

Ghost Sonata - 11

Bed of Nails (Angels) - 13

Mirage - 14

Terrified of My Heart
When it Suddenly Stops - 15

Fleet - 16

Searching for the Missing - 17

Invincible - 18

Dread - 19

**Soft Cell - 20**

**Selective Memory - 21**

**A Picture Says Nothing - 22**

**Coma - 23**

**Future Identity - 24**

**The Act of Believing in Yourself - 25**

**Walking Down The Stairs
of A Place I Don't Want To Be - 26**

**Lost Parts - 27**

**Perch - 28**

**When the Room is All Water - 30**

**Ritual - 31**

**False Idols - 32**

**ABOUT WITCH DOCTOR - 33**

## Diorama

Motion in miniatures

how do we talk about how she walks
on lacquered lain floors
among pliable pieces?

Stash the heart in the ground
try to remember there is life all around.

Definitive statements turn us vacant.  Never know what to
call it.
Tame human arrangement, sleep-state stills, portraits in
portions.
But
we can place them, slide, stick, push them in -
do what I want.
Give them Free Will.

Stab the heart in the ground.

The meanings lost or unheard of, the physical will still
exist.

How do you see it all?
The living sets,
steady legs enter the mist.

# King

You were solid gold back then
You were gold just like a king

Now, a weak matter
 the creeping and the crawl.
Do we like this? Do it like this.
Panic at its peak
havoc manifest
celebrate its grief, eventually, someone has to come.
Leave it alone
let it hit home
like a hammer to the head.
How does it feel? It feels like this.
Systematic images
the first sign of falling buildings
failing reliability
the funeral and the memories.

## Special Guests

Demure, ill-fitting master of disguise
Devoted to you
to all face value
Yet there is nothing I'm seeing
that I truly believe
The way shadows shower
cellar walls, floors, doors
bleeding and healing
Emaciated figures sucked in surfaces
An extension, presence projector-a mute second skin
smooth human pools
whose context is never clear
Like fire
like pain
like dreams
like drugs
The rest is pure heartlessness
and what follows, our shadows-
dark, vacant compassion
tonight
and in morning,
in light
and in mourning.

## Grave Gang

Dreaming colors, I like everything I see
skies are screaming
so we take pictures
of rust, luster and greens.

Blood above, be one buried beneath,
beyond borders and logic's scope
where fate plays no part
holds no cards.
Distant Sixes
spare no heart
lifting off, leaving us
The lowering tradition, candlelit vigil
The clamor of souls
in air we don't see, freedom we won't feel.
Immense Death hovering over cement
Immune -
arms crossed over chest.

## Only Annual

We still keep boxes
colors and other
viewfinders
I'm thinking mostly numbers
in days, how I've slept
in far
in few
I did something like this once
I wonder about your heart

Fireworks, eyes up
on days off calendars
the x's over squares
nails at each end
extend, extend.

We make the best
of waking from nightmares
You astound me
like comfort - hovering doves
You make reality calmer -
softer than dreams
awaking on impact...
it throws us down
a forward snap -
a trap, you set.

We still keep boxes
maybe talk -
only annual,
listen for details and disconnect.

## Ghost Sonata

Silhouettes are my favorite. Just dark, with no heart
behind it.
No burn no puncture no break. No breath no eyes no soul
to take…

Removed from tombs
roots of blueprints
grids, I've imagined
lines and other things
tight, white, passive
legs aggressive
intertwined and
pacing space.
Fingertips rip,
pinpricks
drill bits
tracing my skin
digging
'til its pulp,
soft, purple and sick.

They could be ghosts by now
frozen in being alone
envy in rising kites
infinite isolation
haunting halls
walking through walls
waiting for it to wind their limbs
spinning pinwheel
if they like it
then they will.
Eyes evaporate
liquids confining to caskets
cozy-bodied bat
beaten
buried in backyards.
Skeletons
apparitions
seen
bare in the breeze
vanishing…
hanging, swinging, from trees.

## Bed of Nails (Angels)


Pay them to sleep
pay them to eat
pay them for patterns
pay them to repeat
"apple - blue - shoes"
now say it back to me.
Take a look at my blood
take a look at my face
it is science
this paralysis
a bed of nails for balance
amputating senses
lowering defenses
what is a soul to do
but find its soul solution
at all
in anything
it is sensible to speed
like you've got wings.

## Mirage

mirage,
I remember you painfully
on damp, cherry wood
arms and legs strewn about - sticking to slivers
air thick like glue
as it was
I was red and cut down
appearing not to notice
though we all knew it...

Her jaws were sharp
eyes too
of mid-June pools
the very sight submerges
and swims with sharks
swallowing a thousand leagues
to sing me static but serene.

Trusting what I saw
I stood by and watched
her bats' black silhouette
translate her body language
better than any conversation
we ever could have had.

By now the fire had flooded
the smoke climbed clouds up
morphing against the sky, things I wanted to see.

**Terrified of My Heart**
**When it Suddenly Stops**

The death of one is staying
suspended and ahead of me.
Squeezing innards inward,
a pause in the claws
to execute the other.

If it were any surprise
I'd learned to cope this time
committing to all illusion
I will be fine.
If I do not look around me
surrounding, solitary
this bloodless, bursting, breathtaking
peril.

## Fleet

I would like to do this on my own.
So then what do I do with you?
Carve a declaration, mean it this time.
Blow away the excess -
dispersing sawdust, let it descend.
Sprawling matters
in this shrinking situation.
Wash it off, the waters warm.
Reluctant, disappearing smears.
Hand over hand. There, it's gone.

I'm afraid there will be more like you.
Heels sinking, forward steps coming for me.
Infinite changelings inserting themselves
in places I've repressed.
We'll go on living like that
that's why I've done this.

A private mission
where every place is a silent church.
Panting like an animal, a fire underneath.
You sit in sleepless rooms blowing out smoke.
Burning, bottling, building a bomb.
Never resting easy thinking of me.
As I smolder in another - my breathing heavy.
Your mind detonates.
Out, it puts me.

## Searching for the Missing


Run amok pent-up octopus
searching for a murky hand
in the grips of a globular swamp
sweeping for skin like a zombie alligator
pulling by the neck,
what goes through his head?
Dirt in the fingernails, lines in the palms -
let us remember the way you were.

Force any covered corpse to mean more.
Dents where the bones intersect.
The monsters that caused it...
The paralysis of fingerprints, gathering evidence
 firmly pressed around metal cylinders
like spiders' legs-nimble pins and needles
Spinning silk webs, beds of symmetry,
beds of death. The most comforting kind of horrific.

Mindful, multiple personality
I know you're not real
I know you're not there
I  think that's exciting
I think that's crazy…

## Invincible

Rise up like doves' blaring white wings
gravitational unrest -
we can't talk about this so I talk to myself.


"I don't know how to talk about this..."
into mirrors I confess.
Punishers striking,
smearing the closeness of my face
things I shouldn't second guess
how anonymous it most likely is.


You will lie to me for safety
crystal teeth to my  ears
that is how I'll see through
all of your ten heads.

## Dread

There is nothing for you now
Yet you've shown no restraint
That inevitable bleak will be so heavy, I hope
When you take and take,

Taken so much for granted
and now you miss it, I know.

But it's you whose lost it.
An anxious, irrational heap
cracking down the middle,
 an endless crushing stream, meticulous mining.
Digging you up, sharp and piercing your spirit.

Make a morgue of your organs
and fucking live with it.

## Soft Cell

If I've ever described anything to you as perfect as this
then I loved you far too much in perfection
and not enough for how you truly exist.

Channeling so much between us
standing stark and severe
Together to tell the others
of a time when we've never felt so real

Usually kept in closets
deposits in boxes with bows.
Killing enclosed, claustrophobic
crevices in corners with holes.

Once the property prevailed, sprouting up around us,
an addition to the captivity, we've bloomed by its bars.

Swimming to sleep it off, dripping painful pins and
needles.
A fire's failed darkness with hell around the corner.

Thriving without a center
 no hush in hiding spots
certainly no bravery, just contorting towards comfort.
Awaiting altitudes to dismember, biting winds to butcher
a halt on old sentences,
a halt on all progress
a grave that I visit, but never care to reminisce.

## Selective Memory

Petals on pages
 boiled my blood
 ate away my sleep

Soaking sonnets unconscious,
ink on love letters,
little things we'll never get over.
Written with broken wrists,
familiar phrases
past success.

When fire has no influence
neither dirt nor death
How I choose to look back
can mean more than events.

## A Picture Says Nothing

Your portrait is not practical,
its fragile like porcelain
a damaging demeanor
pronouncing permanent and sullen.
Not far from the frozen fix
in other stiff shots
if you look affected in future albums,
I'd mistake you for someone else.
The dark room was unlocked,
pictures suspended on a line
illustrating inanimate behavior
what the developer implies.
Do away with the defects:
set my eye color right,
cut you out completely,
notify my mind that you've died.
Though the still shot remains
an arm adhered  around my shoulder
like you never really left
we never got older.
I deciphered a thousand words,
which together spoke louder.
This is the only way to speak to you,
telepathically through a picture.
Unable to blink  in a photo
let alone
look upon you in person.
Barely a replica of the reality
a portrayal of affairs,
a flash the only indication
we were ever there.

## Coma

I watch the women in water
the arcs their bodies make
they don't do that anywhere else

 I am lustful for the part in your hair
it'll stay that way
soaked at the bottom of the ocean,
when you come up for air -
salted, heavy and cold, like a stone.
The flips, twists of your legs, as you float.

*Do not wake up*
*Never forget.*

You want me in there with you
I can tell
because you pull me in so hard -
"Don't pretend you don't want it,"
tell me I've taken too long.

Pretending not to see from where
I could see everything.
I told you I was going to leave,
looked back, and there was no one following.

I know now there is no choice
You are predetermined
A detriment
A dream

## Future Identity

I knew somebody I saw outside of me
You are all those sentimental things I think about
abuse at its best
to give and get nothing
You'd be surprised
how good it feels.


They're all laughing
but I can say I see what you do not
You'd be surprised
how good it feels to be wrong.

I knew I saw somebody outside of me
sitting there while my future is fucking leaving
being sucked out every second
How do I let my body betray me?

## The Act of Believing in Yourself

You hear it everywhere
like a gong, something irritating
hard to take and won't shut off.

I think it's a spectacle when said out loud
like we've all got golden skeletons.
I don't.
"Let's talk about that," the therapist says.

Call a doctor
Call a meeting
whatever you can set-up.
Build it -
whatever makes you believe.
Then, pull out the
                    middle brick.

Immerse yourself in this missing layer,
not a casket, but an easy place to rest.

## Walking Down The Stairs
## of A Place I Don't Want To Be

There is so much beneath the floor
yelling up
the tremors that beg you down
but you don't want to come

a blood feast
if you didn't know better
 too late
body slipping inside the future

too bare for anyone down here.

I worry about bear traps and swinging hooks
because what's the difference
when you're nervous.

It is good to forget about the grave
hand pounding up through dirt
head on a stick,
separate yourself

the need to be weightless
it is good to forget about the body
chainsaw down the torso,
separate yourself

when the zombie ravages your brain
it's good to be thoughtless
Become the Big Bad -
separate                yourself.

## Lost Parts

When both of you are around
one fleshes me out
 and one makes me a skeleton,
 doesn't remember my conditions
or the side effects.
Rubbing together, they scrape - make horrible sounds,
they don't know how to *live* together.

Wishing to reanimate
shrink reality
count what I can't find and try like Hell to pull it close to
me.
I hope those parts meet halfway
and if they do not -
It will work against the headway
the name I've made.

Hope those parts will come crawling back
like Evil Dead, putty and caked
reattach and begin again.

## Perch

We are removing something the body has come to rely on
so come to the funeral where the rest of us get to live.
The room looks slant and overgrown not upright and
meaningful.

Pops of my chest let you know I am alive and sorry
for all of the things you saw during my death.

Descending melodies calm me - put us to sleep
liquid needle anesthesia.

 Add me to the reverie
where we forget
I sink inside the ground.

But if I'm not floating over buildings or joining Angels in
song
does that mean you won't know where to find me?

Cut my teeth for ivory - get what you can.
Reap the satin, velvet aches and pains,
birds in cages, they won't keep
in a coffin.

Remember to save every stain.
Naming new keepsakes only death can make relevant
so my relatives can relate to me.

I want to see them so badly.

Rouse exhausted heart
rise vapor and smoke,
postpone the vanishing
the pause in a trapdoor.

## When the Room is All Water

I believed in it so much I knew I would never be on its
level
resting under the folds of reality
siphoning all fear and fascination
superstitions that scare off future plans
while the actual doctor
drains
your
pain
filling bags of blood
bleeding them into you


Split it so it pools,
spill it 'til your lungs stretch
'til it's up to your neck

When the room is all water
flood the body

unsure which will appear first, keep an open mind
fill it 'til it bursts

No leverage in the undertow

an unbearable fate so above average,
only in my mind do you levitate.

**Ritual**


Halos with hanging candles
metal cradles to catch the wax
blocks of bodies stacked upright
climbing smoky hills
where the spirit sits tracing its own outline
anxious, transparent and passing through hands.

You are
Two different beings
Here and Underneath

Blood and black magic
grinded colored sands
prayer and poison vials
the evil and conjure that bring dead to life.

Unearthed, unnatural; lurking ghost, walking -
anxious, transparent and passing through hands.

**False Idols**

There are many of us who will not sleep through this:

White sheets over every head
where we are not well

Untrustworthy indicators
pulse pressure and perspiration
promise no miracle here

Glowing eyes on the other side
Various,  Imaginary...
                                    Beasts, Breathing

It is the loudest thing,
sounds of hearts pounding, endlessly...

Need more time to get out alive.

Red skies pushing in the ground
fire falling, burning up, spreading the earth.

An apocalyptic moment
 your head bringing you back.

We need more time to die.

Day in and day out
the motion that makes you minuscule.

**JESSICA ROUGEAU** shares and discusses her journey and the inspiration for *Witch Doctor:*

"Writing this book was a form of recovery for me. On May 25, 2010, I went into cardiac arrest; my heart gave out and I was declared dead for what I heard was 10 minutes. I woke up a couple of weeks later in the hospital, my memory literally erased of the events leading up to the collapse. Until that point I had not been admitted to a hospital since the day I was born, never broke a bone, and rarely ever got sick. I feel incredibly lucky to have not suffered any brain damage, but I remember the moment the surgeon slipped that tiny metal device under my skin, over my heart. I was to learn shortly after that I had something called Tachychardia, and the device implanted inside my chest was a defibrillator. This little machine would combat my extremely fast heart rate during moments when the electrical signals in my heart's upper chambers fired abnormally. The reality of this life-changing event was not something I allowed myself to process right away. I do not think I let myself be terrified by this, even initially, and I wish that I could have told myself it was okay to be scared.

Upon leaving the hospital and hoping to return to my life as normal, I was suddenly immersed in the reality of taking meds every day and attending countless doctors' visits and follow-ups. During those first few months, the realization that none of this was going away made it difficult not to let the trauma overtake me. So it did.

I was in the doctor's office one day and there was an article posted on a cabinet as I was waiting alone in the exam room. It said something like 99% of people afflicted with the condition I have die because the ambulance does not get there in time. From then on, I really let myself have it. I convinced myself I did not deserve to be in that near-impossible surviving percentage because I felt I had nothing to offer anyone.

Though never diagnosed, I feel I suffered heavily from PTSD and ignored the thought of speaking to a therapist about the issues I could not fully come to terms with. My anxiety was increased and the worst part was I could not filter any of my emotions into creative energy. Something I had always been able to do in the past.

The shining light through all of this was horror, which sounds insane. But being on bed rest for two months gave me hours of down time to watch my favorite horror films and tv shows. Beyond my friends and family, who are the main reason I pulled through, when they weren't around I had another outlet. And thought it was a long road, I eventually regained my positive spirit and creative energy.

Horror content has always inspired and excited me. Ever since I was a young kid. I have always written poetry and shortly after I started feeling like myself again, it became difficult not to let the inspiration overtake me. So it did.

I used some older material I had written previously, re-worked themes, and then began pouring out all of this new poetry that said so precisely what I had always wanted to say, but never could. Writing this collection was therapeutic and unbelievably fulfilling. I have rarely liked my work in the past and with this collection I am so excited to share it with others.

The title of this book so perfectly conveys my entire journey. It blends my love of writing horror themed work with the challenges I have faced medically and all of the moments I felt scared and completely out of control. I wanted to create a different meaning for the term witch doctor while still very much incorporating the original definition. The idea of healing powers, protection and divination, this type of magic that witch doctors are known for, stands to classify the purpose for this collection. Writing became an alternative healing to get my mind back together and overcome what I never thought I would.

I credit all of my physical and mental recovery to my family, friends and *Witch Doctor* "